What's in the Cupbo[ard]

Teacher's Book

by Janet Warburton
Pupil's Book by Stan Cullimore

Contents

Section 1: for Below Average Readers
Guided reading and writing lessons using:
Toy Cupboard and *Art Cupboard*

Teaching Notes for Guided Reading (session 1)	2
Teaching Notes for Guided Reading (session 2)	3
Teaching Notes for Guided Writing (session 1)	4
Teaching Notes for Guided Writing (session 2)	5
Copymaster 1: using captions	6
Copymaster 2: using captions	7
Copymaster 3: making a list	8
Copymaster 4: making a list	9

Section 2: for Average Readers
Guided reading and writing lessons using:
Dressing Up Cupboard and *PE Cupboard*

Teaching Notes for Guided Reading (session 1)	10
Teaching Notes for Guided Reading (session 2)	11
Teaching Notes for Guided Writing (session 1)	12
Teaching Notes for Guided Writing (session 2)	13
Copymaster 5: using captions	14
Copymaster 6: using captions	15
Copymaster 7: writing captions	16
Copymaster 8: writing a caption	17

Section 3: for Above Average Readers
Guided reading and writing lessons using:
Food Cupboard and *Tool Cupboard*

Teaching Notes for Guided Reading (session 1)	18
Teaching Notes for Guided Reading (session 2)	19
Teaching Notes for Guided Writing (session 1)	20
Teaching Notes for Guided Writing (session 2)	21
Copymaster 9: using captions	22
Copymaster 10: using captions	23
Copymaster 11: writing instructions	24
Copymaster 12: writing instructions/captions	25

Edinburgh Gate
Harlow, Essex

What's in the Cupboard? Year 1 Term 1 Section **1** Below Average Level

Toy Cupboard and Art Cupboard

Guided Reading (session 1)

Key Objectives
- Read and use captions, e.g. labels on equipment.
- Reinforce and apply word-level skills through guided reading.

Introduction

- Ask children to flick quickly through the whole book and then to look at the front page and read the title. *What kind of book do you think this is? Is it a story book? How can you tell?*
- Look through it more slowly. *What kind of information could you find out from this book? How might it be useful?* [To find things, put them back in the right place, to know what they are called.]
- Ask children to turn to page 2 and explain that you are going to read Section 1, about the toy cupboard and the art cupboard.
- **Strategy Check:** Recap the range of contextual and phonic strategies the children know. Ask them to look at the toys on page 2 and read their labels. *Which words have the same sound at the beginning? Are there any words with the same sound at the end? Do any of these words have shorter words hidden inside them? How might this help you if you get stuck on a word?*

Reading and Discussion

- Ask children to read pages 4 and 5 alone. Explain that when they have read them, you will want to know the name of the teddy bear and the age of the van.
- Look at the art cupboard on page 6 and discuss where in school the children might see all those things, before reading the list of words alone. Again comment on issues to develop skills of blending and segmenting. *Find the words that have the same two phonemes at the beginning. Do you know any other words starting with 'gl'? Look carefully at 'glue'. What other word can you make if you change the first letter? Are there any others?*
- Ask children to find out more about some of these objects by reading the sentences on pages 8 and 9. *What does glue do to your fingers? What does glitter look like?*

Returning to the Text for Evaluation and Analysis

- Return to the two questions for each cupboard and discuss the ideas.
- *Look carefully at the layout of the pages. How is the information on pages 2 and 3 written differently from pages 6 and 7? Why? When has the author used just words? When has he used sentences? Why?*
- Direct children to page 10 and ask them if they can remember the toys that were on the shelf. Ask them to read the page to themselves to see if they had remembered them all and then repeat for page 11.

© Pearson Education Limited 2004

What's in the Cupboard? Year 1 Term 1   Section ❶ Below Average Level

Toy Cupboard and Art Cupboard

Guided Reading (session 2)

Key Objectives
- Read and use captions, e.g. labels on equipment.
- Reinforce and apply word-level skills through guided reading.

Each pair of children will need Copymaster ❶ and a set of toys/labels cut out from Copymaster ❷ (all preferably laminated), and reusable adhesive.

The teacher will need enlarged copies of Copymaster ❶ and Copymaster ❷.

Introduction
- Remind children of their reading in the previous session. *What were the two cupboards used for? Can you remember any of the toys in the cupboard? What was the most useful thing in the art cupboard? What do you like to use best?*
- Explain that today they can fill the toy cupboard themselves, but that they must then make sure everything has the right label or caption.
- **Strategy Check:** Recap the range of contextual and phonic strategies the children know, especially those that they practised in the last session.

Reading and Discussion
- Show children the enlarged copy of Copymaster ❶ – an empty cupboard – and the cutout toys and labels from Copymaster ❷. Model for them filling the shelves [arranging the toys how they would like] and then reading out and attaching the labels. [You may wish to make links with the Numeracy Strategy by emphasising positional language.]
- Ask children to work in pairs to organise and label their own toy cupboards.
- When the cupboards are organised, ask children to read through the labels again for accuracy.
- Finally, read and attach the sentence-long captions near to the appropriate objects.

Returning to the Text for Evaluation and Analysis
- Ask children why it is useful to have these labels and captions. *Why is it good to have a label outside the cupboard?* [So you know what's in it.] *Why are the caption sentences useful? What might happen if the label didn't say the ball is hard? What if someone new came to stay in your house? How would the labels help them?* [Tell them the bear's name, etc.]
- Check that everyone has used the labels to sort their cupboards out appropriately and that objects have the right labels attached.
- Review and praise children for the particular strategies they used to solve problems in their reading.

© Pearson Education Limited 2004

What's in the Cupboard?   Year 1 Term 1   Section ❶ Below Average Level

Toy Cupboard

Guided Writing (session 1)

Key Objectives
- Make simple lists.
- Spell common irregular words and write CVC words accurately.

Task
Children will make a list of the contents of their own toy cupboard at home, so that they can check all the toys are there.

Each child will need Copymaster ❸.
The teacher will need an enlarged copy of Copymaster ❸.

Introduction
- Remind children of the book from their guided reading session and the work done to complete their own 'cupboards'.
- Look at the picture on page 2 together and point out to children the gaps on the shelves of toys. *If this were your cupboard at home, what else would you want to put in the spaces?*
- Discuss children's own most important/precious/significant toys and get them to decide with a partner on the four extra toys they would put in their cupboard. Ask children to make a note of their ideas on the first part of Copymaster ❸ and model this process on your enlarged copy.

Children Writing Individually
- Using Copymaster ❸, ask children to write the list of what would be in their toy cupboard, including the new and, if they wish, some of the original items. Explain that the list will be pinned outside on the cupboard door, so they know what should be there.
- Remind children to use their independent spelling strategies, especially listening to and segmenting phonemes and their knowledge of other features of words – common patterns, shape, words within words, etc.

Evaluation
- As a group or in pairs check the completed lists, including the new ideas. Discuss how this list will be useful and cut it out to take home and use.
- Discuss the successful spelling strategies that children have used.

Suggested Independent Activities
- Draw and label the items from the list on Copymaster ❸ and add them to the existing cupboards, rereading the labels and thinking about the spelling each time.
- Write stories based on the position of the toys in their cupboard.

© Pearson Education Limited 2004

What's in the Cupboard?   Year 1 Term 1   Section ❶ Below Average Level

Art Cupboard

Guided Writing (session 2)

Key Objectives
- Make simple lists.
- Spell common irregular words and write CVC words accurately.

Task
Children will write a shopping list for the teacher of extra materials they would like to have in the art cupboard.

Each child will need Copymaster ❹.
The teacher will need an enlarged copy of Copymaster ❹.

Introduction
- Remind children of their reading and writing about the toy cupboard and explain that today they are going to think again about the art cupboard.
- Look at page 6 in the book and talk about all the materials they can see. Ask what else they really like to use which isn't already there, e.g. gold stars, gel pens, glitter glue, new brushes.
- Ask children to talk with a partner and decide on no more than four really important items. Ask children to note them on the first part of Copymaster ❹ and model this process on your enlarged copy.
- Remind children to use their independent spelling strategies, especially listening to and segmenting phonemes and their knowledge of other features of words – common patterns, shape, words within words, etc.

Children Writing Individually
- Ask children to think about ideas for extra stock for the art cupboard. Discuss possibilities.
- Using Copymaster ❹, model for children the process of writing a shopping list, 'thinking aloud' as you do it.
- Ask children then to write you a shopping list, including their new ideas and any items from the original cupboard that they think they need more of.
- Remind children to use their independent spelling strategies when writing.

Evaluation
- Ask children what they think would happen if you made a special trip to the art shop in town with their lists and then found you couldn't read them when you got there. Emphasise the purpose of the list, which is not to look attractive, but to be very clear.
- Evaluate the list against those criteria.
- Note: It may help children's understanding that writing always has a purpose if you are able to acquire one or two items from their lists for the classroom.

Suggested Independent Activities
- Draw and label the items from the shopping list on Copymaster ❹ and add them to the existing cupboards, rereading the labels and thinking about the spelling each time.
- Compile a list of items from the cupboard needed to make an extravagant birthday card.

© Pearson Education Limited 2004

In the Cupboard

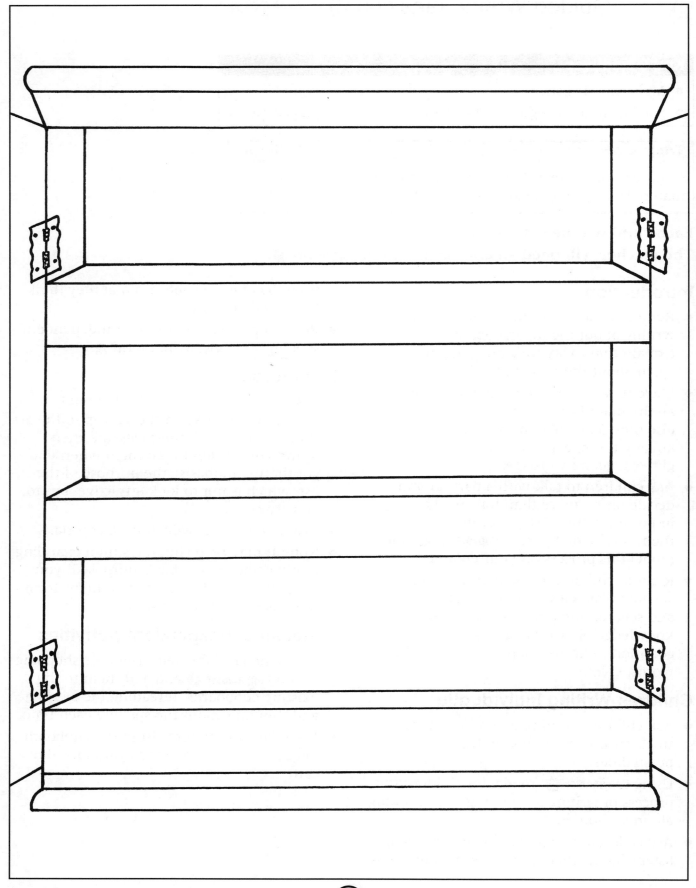

Toy Cupboard

train	teddy bear	van
bat	ball	robot

This teddy bear is called Fred.

This robot can walk.

This van is ten years old.

This ball is very hard.

What's in the Cupboard? Copymaster 3 Toy Cupboard

Making Lists: Toys

My own favourite toys:

_____   _____

_____   _____

My Toys

_____

_____

_____

_____

_____

_____

_____

_____

What's in the Cupboard?   Copymaster 4   **Art Cupboard**

Making Lists: Art Materials

Things I like to use most:

_____   _____

_____   _____

Shopping List

_____

_____

_____

_____

_____

_____

_____

What's in the Cupboard?   Year 1 Term 1   Section 2   Average Level

Dressing Up Cupboard

Guided Reading (session 1)

Key Objectives

- Read and use captions, e.g. labels on equipment.
- Reinforce and apply word-level skills through guided reading.
- Use awareness of the grammar of a sentence to decipher new or unfamiliar words.

Each child will need Copymaster ❶ and a set of items/labels from Copymaster ❺ (preferably laminated), and reusable adhesive.
The teacher will need enlarged copies of Copymaster ❶ and Copymaster ❺.

Introduction

- Ask children to flick quickly through the whole book and then to look at the front page and read the title. *What kind of book do you think this is? Is it a story book? How can you tell? What do we call this kind of book?* Refer to other non-fiction books they have used recently, in classroom displays, etc.
- Look more slowly through all the sections. *What kind of information could you find out from this book? How might it be useful?* [To find things, put them back in the right place, to know what they are called.] *Do we always read this kind of book all the way through?*
- **Strategy Check:** Recap the range of contextual and phonic strategies the children know.

Reading and Discussion

- Ask children to turn to page 12 and explain that you are going to read Section 2 today, about the dressing up cupboard.
- Discuss what they can see on the shelves/rail and then ask them to read the labels by themselves.
- *Which words have the same sound at the beginning? Are there any words with the same sound at the end? Do any of these words have shorter words hidden inside them? Can you find some words that are really two words joined together?*
- Ask children to read pages 14 and 15 alone. *What is the crown made of? How would you feel if you wore the space suit?*

Returning to the Text for Evaluation and Analysis

- Discuss the answers to your two questions, assessing their literal understanding of the text, and include some inferential questions. *If someone were wearing the bridesmaid dress, feather boa, earrings and crown, how would you label them (e.g. princess)?*
- Look carefully at the layout of the pages. *How is the information on pages 14 and 15 written differently from pages 12 and 13? Why? When has the author used just words? When has he used sentences? Why?*
- Ask children if they can remember all the things in the cupboard on page 20, before reading the page alone to see if they were right.
- Show children the cupboard on Copymaster ❶ and the cutout clothes and labels from Copymaster ❺. Model for them filling the shelves [arranging the things how they would like] and then reading out and attaching the labels. [You may wish to make links with the Numeracy Strategy by emphasising positional language.]
- Ask children to fill their cupboard before reading and sticking down the labels. Finally, read and attach the sentence-long captions. Children should exchange 'cupboards' and reread to check for accuracy of labelling.

© Pearson Education Limited 2004

What's in the Cupboard?   Year 1 Term 1   Section ❷   Average Level

PE Cupboard

Guided Reading (session 2)

Key Objectives

- Read and use captions, e.g. labels on equipment.
- Reinforce and apply their word-level skills through guided reading.
- Use awareness of the grammar of a sentence to decipher new or unfamiliar words.

Each child will need **Copymaster ❶** and a set of items/labels from **Copymaster ❻** (preferably laminated), and reusable adhesive.
The teacher will need enlarged copies of **Copymaster ❶** and **Copymaster ❻**.

Introduction

- Remind children of their reading in the previous session. *What was that cupboard used for? Can you remember any of the things in the cupboard?*
- **Strategy Check:** Recap the range of contextual and phonic strategies the children know, particularly those that they used successfully in the last session.

Reading and Discussion

- Explain to the children that they are going to see what is in the PE cupboard, and ask them to look at page 16. Talk about where in school they might see all those things, and ask them to read the list of labels alone.
- Ask children to find out more about some of these things by reading the sentences on pages 18 and 19. *What is the bat used for? Who uses the whistle?*

Returning to the Text for Evaluation and Analysis

- Discuss the answers to your two questions, assessing their literal understanding of the text, and include some inferential questions: *What will happen if you go out to play with the football? Will it be a good game? Why not?*

- Ask children if they can remember all the things in the cupboard on page 21, before reading the page alone to see if they were right.
- Show children the cupboard on **Copymaster ❶** and the cutout equipment and labels from **Copymaster ❻**. Remind them of the work they did on the dressing up cupboard, and ask them to do the same with the PE cupboard.
- Ask children to fill their cupboard before reading and sticking down the labels. Finally, read and attach the sentence-long captions. Children should exchange 'cupboards' with a partner and reread to check for accuracy of labelling.
- Ask children why it is useful to have these labels and captions. *Why is it good to have a label outside the cupboard?* [So you know what's in it.] *Why are the caption sentences useful? What might happen if the caption didn't say the football needs air? What if someone new came to school? How would the labels help them?*

© Pearson Education Limited 2004

What's in the Cupboard? Year 1 Term 1 Section ❷ Average Level

Dressing Up Cupboard

Guided Writing (session 1)

Key Objectives

- Make simple lists.
- Spell common irregular words and write CVC words accurately.
- Write captions and simple sentences for their own work.

Task

Children will design outfits for particular purposes and write captions that explain what they are.

Each child will need Copymaster ❼, scissors and reusable adhesive.
The teacher will need an enlarged copy of Copymaster ❼.

Introduction

- Remind children of the work they did in guided reading. *What was in the dressing up cupboard? Was it just clothes? What else was there? How does it help to have things like sunglasses?*
- Look at the picture on page 12. *To make this the best ever dressing up cupboard, what else would you put in it?*
- Discuss children's ideas and get them to decide with a partner what extra items they would need to dress up a character from a story. Ask children to make a note of their ideas on the first part of Copymaster ❼.
- Remind children to use their independent spelling strategies, especially listening to and segmenting phonemes and their knowledge of other features of words – common patterns, shape, words within words, etc.

Children Writing Individually

- On the second part of Copymaster ❼, ask children to draw the items they thought of and write the accompanying labels.

- Using an enlarged copy of Copymaster ❼, model writing a caption that is a complete sentence. Choose an outfit from the items listed and quickly sketch the character [e.g. a stick figure with cowboy boots, jacket and hat]. Think aloud the options and how you make your choices. *This is a cowboy. This is what a cowboy wears. A cowboy wears boots and a jacket and a special hat.*
- Ask children to write their caption at the bottom of Copymaster ❼.

Evaluation

- As a group discuss the figures and their captions. Talk about whether they give clear information that would be useful to someone else who wanted to be that character.

Suggested Independent Activity

- Design posters to go in your own dressing up cupboard that show and explain, through the captions, how to create particular characters, e.g. 'The princess wears the pink skirt and the crown.'

© Pearson Education Limited 2004

| What's in the Cupboard? | Year 1 Term 1 | Section ❷ | Average Level |

PE Cupboard

Guided Writing (session 2)

Key Objectives

- Write captions and simple sentences for their own work.
- Spell common irregular words and write CVC words accurately.

Task

Children will produce a poster for their school PE cupboard showing what equipment they need for a particular sport, explained in the caption.

Each child will need Copymaster ❽.
The teacher will need an enlarged copy of Copymaster ❽.

Introduction

- Remind children of their reading and writing about the dressing up cupboard, and explain that today they are going to think again about the PE cupboard.
- Look at page 16 in the book and talk about all the equipment they can see. Ask children what they need for particular sports or activities. *What happens if another class has gone off with part of what you need? Is it very annoying?*
- Using the enlarged Copymaster ❽, model for children writing the caption to support a poster showing what is needed for a particular sport.
- Remind children of the independent spelling strategies that they have been using successfully.

Children Writing Individually

- Ask children to sketch their posters quickly and to write an extended caption explaining their problem, using their own copy of Copymaster ❽.

Evaluation

- Explain that successful posters that clearly explain the situation will be put on display by the school PE cupboard to remind everyone of what they should do.
- Evaluate the posters against that criterion.
- Note: It may help children's understanding that writing always has a purpose if you are able to arrange for such a display.

Suggested Independent Activity

- Repeat the activity for a different sport or write a letter to the teacher in charge of PE requesting new/more equipment for your favourite activity.

© Pearson Education Limited 2004

Dressing Up Cupboard

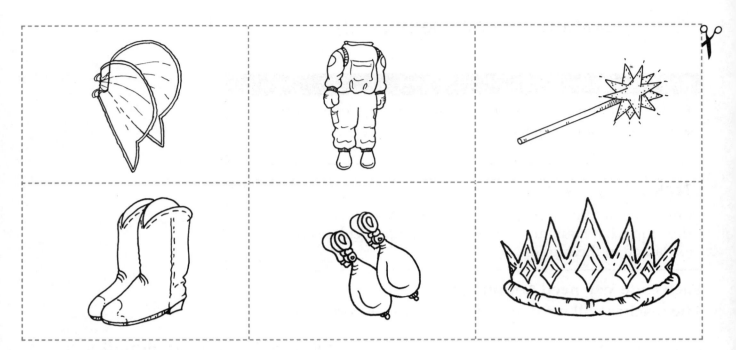

| fairy wings | space suit | magic wand |
| cowboy boots | earrings | crown |

These earrings clip onto your ears.

These cowboy boots go with the hat.

This crown is made of plastic.

These fairy wings go with the pink dress.

This magic wand lights up.

This space suit is hot to wear.

PE Cupboard

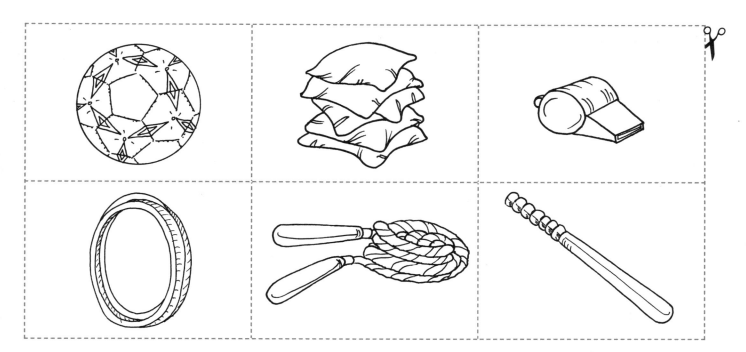

| football | beanbags | whistle |
| hoops | skipping rope | bat |

| The teacher uses this whistle. |
| This skipping rope is long. |
| This is a rounders bat. |
| This football needs some more air inside it. |
| Hoops are made of plastic. |
| Beanbags are easy to catch. |

What's in the Cupboard? Copymaster **7** Dressing up Cupboard

Dressing Up Cupboard

Extra clothes:

_____   _____

_____   _____

Your caption:

_____

_____

_____

Playing Sport

When we play _____
we need _____, _____
and _____

Please _____

What's in the Cupboard? Year 1 Term 1 Section ❸ Above Average Level

Food Cupboard

Guided Reading (session 1)

Key Objectives
- Read and use captions, e.g. labels on equipment.
- Reinforce and apply word-level skills through guided reading.
- Use awareness of the grammar of a sentence to decipher new or unfamiliar words.

Each child will need Copymaster ❶ and a set of items/labels from Copymaster ❾ (preferably laminated), and reusable adhesive.
The teacher will need enlarged copies of Copymaster ❶ and Copymaster ❾.

Introduction
- Ask children to flick quickly through the whole book and then to look at the cover and read the title. *What kind of book do you think this is? Is it a story book? How can you tell? What do we call this kind of book?* Refer to other non-fiction books they have used recently, in classroom displays, etc.
- Invite children to look more slowly through all the sections. *What kind of information could you find out from this book? How might it be useful?* [To find things, put them back in the right place and to know what they are called.]
- **Strategy Check:** Recap the range of contextual and phonic strategies the children know. Encourage them to look for words with the same sounds at the beginning and at the end.

Reading and Discussion
- Ask children to turn to page 22 and explain that you are going to read Section 3 today, about the food cupboard.
- Discuss what they can see on the shelves and then ask them to read the labels by themselves.
- Talk together about any difficult words, pointing out letter patterns, and highlighting issues that will develop children's skills in blending and segmenting. *Which words have the same sound at the beginning? Are there any words with the same sound at the end? Do any of these words have shorter words hidden inside them?*
- Ask children to find out more about this selection of food by reading pages 24 and 25 alone. *Where do the onions come from? What fruit is used to make the jam?*

Returning to the Text for Evaluation and Analysis
- Discuss the answers to your two questions and include some inferential questions. *Which food would you choose for a quick snack? Which things would be no use to you if there were no electricity?*
- Look carefully at the layout of the pages. *How is the information on pages 24 and 25 written differently from pages 22 and 23? Why? When has the author used just words? When has he used sentences? Why?*
- Direct children to page 30 and ask them if they can remember the things that were in the cupboard. Ask them to read the page again to see if they remembered them all.
- Show children the enlarged copy of Copymaster ❶ and the cutout food items and labels from Copymaster ❾. Model for them filling the shelves and then reading out and attaching the labels.
- Ask children to fill their cupboard before reading and sticking down the labels. Finally, read and attach the sentence-long captions near to the appropriate objects. Children should exchange 'cupboards' and reread to check for accuracy of labelling.

© Pearson Education Limited 2004

What's in the Cupboard?   Year 1 Term 1   Section ❸ Above Average Level

Tool Cupboard

 Guided Reading (session 2)

Key Objectives

- Read and use captions, e.g. labels on equipment.
- Reinforce and apply their word-level skills through guided reading.
- Use awareness of the grammar of a sentence to decipher new or unfamiliar words.

Each child will need Copymaster ❶ and a set of items/labels from Copymaster ❿ (preferably laminated), and reusable adhesive. The teacher will need enlarged copies of Copymaster ❶ and Copymaster ❿.

Introduction

- Remind children of their reading in the previous session. *What was that cupboard used for? Can you remember any of the things in the cupboard?*
- **Strategy Check:** Recap the range of contextual and phonic strategies the children know, particularly those that they used in the last session.

Reading and Discussion

- Explain that today they are going to see what is in the tool cupboard and ask them to look at page 26. Talk about where at school or at home they might see all those things. Ask them to read the list of labels alone.
- Ask children to find out more about some of these tools by reading the sentences on pages 28 and 29. *What is the glue used for? What makes the drill work?*

Returning to the Text for Evaluation and Analysis

- Discuss the answers to your two questions, assessing their literal understanding of the text, and include some inferential questions: *Which tools would you choose to mend a chair leg with? Would you choose sticky tape? Would the screws and a hammer be all right? Would the nails and a screwdriver make the chair strong enough? Why not?*

- Ask children if they can remember all the things in the cupboard on page 31, before reading the page alone to see if they were right.
- Show children the cupboard on Copymaster ❶ and the cutout tools and labels from Copymaster ❿. Remind them of the work they did on the food cupboard, and explain that you want them to do the same with the tool cupboard.
- Ask children to fill their cupboard, before reading and sticking down the labels. Finally, read and attach the sentence-long captions. Children should exchange 'cupboards' with a partner and reread to check for accuracy of labelling.
- Ask children why it is useful to have these labels and captions. *Why is it good to have a label outside the cupboard?* [So you know what's in it.] *Why are the caption sentences useful? What might happen if the caption didn't say the glue is for sticking wood? What if a visitor came to stay? How would the captions help them?*

© Pearson Education Limited 2004

What's in the Cupboard?   Year 1 Term 1   Section ❸ Above Average Level

Food Cupboard

Guided Writing (session 1)

Key Objectives

- Write captions for their own work.
- Write and draw simple instructions and labels for everyday classroom use.
- Spell common irregular words and write CVC words accurately.

Task

Children will write recipes/instructions for making a meal, using the ingredients in the food cupboard.

Each child will need Copymaster ⓫ and sticky notes.
The teacher will need an enlarged copy of Copymaster ⓫.

Introduction

- Remind children of the work they did in guided reading. *What was in the cupboard we read about? What kind of food? Was it all in tins? Was it all raw? Did all of it need to be cooked?*

- Look at the picture on page 22 and 23. Talk through the different categories of food – vegetables, tins, drinks, snacks, sauces, etc. Talk about any favourite foods that are not in the cupboard and ask children to sketch/label a few of the most important ones on sticky notes to add to the shelves in the picture.

- Explain that their task is to choose a meal they would like to eat from the items in the cupboard and to write instructions [a recipe] for how they would like it to be made, e.g. a jam sandwich, a cup of tea.

- Using the enlarged **Copymaster ⓫**, model writing the instructions, talking aloud about the layout [a list followed by sentences] and the decisions that need to be made. *I'm going to do beans on toast because I love that, so I need in my list – beans, bread, tomato ketchup. I'll need some butter – that's not in the cupboard. Now I have to think what to do first.*

- Remind children to use their independent spelling strategies, especially listening to and segmenting phonemes and their knowledge of other features of words – common patterns, shape, words within words, etc.

Children Writing Individually

- Ask children to write their own recipe on **Copymaster ⓫**. Encourage them to plan what they are going to make, and to think through the ingredients and steps before they write each one.

- Encourage oral rehearsal of each sentence before writing it.

Evaluation

- Choose one recipe to carry out in the classroom and follow the instructions exactly, noting anything which causes a problem. Ask children to evaluate each other's recipes for clarity and accuracy.

- Invite parents or another class to follow the instructions and to write an evaluation themselves, to be shared with the group.

Suggested Independent Activity

- Experiment with writing recipes for more dishes using further copies of **Copymaster ⓫** as a model. Illustrate the recipes and label the illustrations clearly.

© Pearson Education Limited 2004

What's in the Cupboard? Year 1 Term 1 Section ❸ Above Average Level

Tool Cupboard

Guided Writing (session 2)

Key Objectives

- Write captions for their own work.
- Write and draw simple instructions and labels for everyday classroom use.
- Spell common irregular words and write CVC words accurately.

Task

Children will create a safety poster to be displayed on the door of the school tool cupboard, using captions to give instructions and advice for safe use of tools.

Each child will need Copymaster ⑫.
The teacher will need an enlarged copy of Copymaster ⑫.

Introduction

- Remind children of their reading and writing about the food cupboard, and explain that today they are going to think again about the tool cupboard.
- Look at page 26 in the book and talk about all the equipment they can see. Ask children what they need for particular activities, e.g. making a junk model, puppets, a doll's bed, a toy playground swing. Remind children of any recent activities in Design and Technology or Science. Talk about what the particular tools do and the correct ways to use them.
- Explain that they are going to create some posters to go on the school tool cupboard to make sure that everyone uses the tools correctly and safely.
- Using the enlarged Copymaster ⑫, model for children the writing of captions and instructions, emphasising the need to sort out your ideas in order and to plan sentences before writing.
- Remind children of the independent spelling strategies that they have been using successfully, and point out to them the capital letters and full stops that demarcate your sentences.

Children Writing Individually

- Ask children to use your model and the frame on Copymaster ⑫ to create their own poster. Remind them that they also have the text in the book as a word bank, and that the purpose of this kind of poster is to give very clear information.

Evaluation

- Invite the teacher in charge of Design and Technology to visit the group and review the posters in terms of the accuracy of information, clarity of presentation, and helpfulness in persuading others to take proper care with the tools.
- Note: It may help children's understanding that writing always has a purpose if you are able to arrange for an appropriate display.

Suggested Independent Activities

- Complete the posters with more care and add additional illustrations with captions.
- Use further copies of Copymaster ⑫ to write about the use of different tools.

© Pearson Education Limited 2004

Food Cupboard

| tomato ketchup | baked beans | pasta |
| onions | crisps | tea bags |

There are 160 tea bags in this box.

Tomato ketchup is very thick.

You cook this pasta for six minutes.

This is strawberry jam.

These onions come from Spain.

These are cheese and onion crisps.

You can eat baked beans on toast.

This is sliced bread.

Tool Cupboard

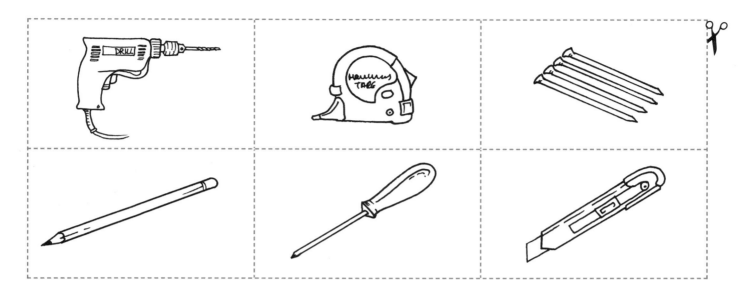

| drill | tape measure | nails |
| pencil | screwdriver | knife |

This hammer is very heavy.

This knife is very sharp.

This pencil is not very sharp.

This tape measure is six metres long.

You can stick wood with this glue.

This screwdriver is for small screws.

This drill is electric.

These nails are six centimetres long.

My Favourite Meal

How to make _____

You will need: _____

_____

_____

_____

First, you _____
Then you _____
Next, you _____
At the end you _____
_____

It will taste _____